A WELLBEING JOURNEY

GRADE 5

Title: A Wellbeing Journey Grade 5
ISBN: 9781957136936

Editors: Janna Nobleza and Elisa Flammini

Published 2023 by Seltrove, an imprint of Edtrove

TABLE OF CONTENTS

SKILLS MAP

Self-Awareness

Social Awareness

Self-Management

Responsible Decision-making

Relationship Skills

Discussion Questions

Hello!

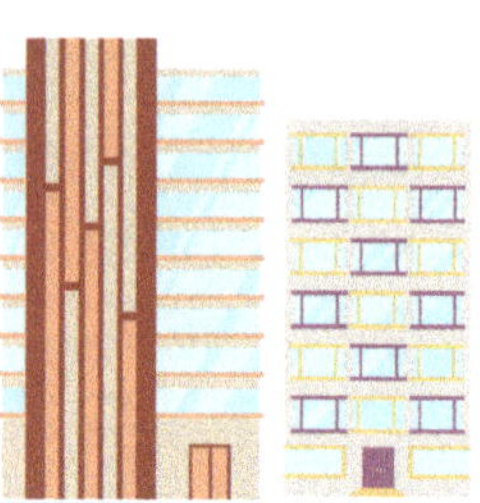

Wellbeing focuses on who you are as an individual and your relationships you have with the people and world around you.

Research shows that people who build strong skills in the areas of social and emotional wellbeing are

- more likely to succeed in school
- better able to make responsible, healthy decisions
- more positive and have an optimistic look on life

To begin, simply pick a journal prompt, activity, or project based on the amount of time you have to spend.

Looking for more guidance? Our Teacher Guide and Parent Guide can help. Find it at www.myibsource.com.

Fill in Your Personal Info

YOUR NAME: ______________________________

YOUR BIRTHDAY: __________________________

YOUR SELF-PORTRAIT

Setting Goals

Let's set some goals for our personal growth this year in the areas of Academics, Reading, Passion, and Wellness.

1

Start by brainstorming in a small group possible goals for each category. You want your goals to be specific so you know exactly what you are working on, and measurable. Measurable means you can tell if you meet the goal.

Here are some examples of specific and measurable goals:

1. I will be able to read the Merlin Missions books from The Magic Treehouse by quarter 2.
2. I will know how to introduce myself in French and know all the colors by winter break.
3. I will enter my artwork in the school competition this year.

2

Now that you have brainstormed possible goals for each category with classmates, take some quiet time to write your goals below. They can be similar to the group's brainstorming goal, or they can be different.

Academic Goal

I will be able to____

By the time of_________________________.

I will Reach this goal by ___________________________________

____

I am excited to work on this goal because _________________________

____

____

Reading Goal

I will be able to____

By the time of_________________________.

I will Reach this goal by ___________________________________

____

I am excited to work on this goal because _________________________

____

____

Passion Goal

I will be able to____

By the time of_______________________________.

I will Reach this goal by ____________________________________

____

I am excited to work on this goal because ___________________________

____

____

Wellness Goal

I will be able to____

By the time of_______________________________.

I will Reach this goal by ____________________________________

____

I am excited to work on this goal because ___________________________

____

____

GOAL CHECK-IN

Look back at the goals you set for yourself at the beginning of the year.

Add notes to check-in or make changes to your goals. It's ok to add or change your goals a little, but keep pushing yourself to grow this year. If you feel you have met your goal, make a new goal for yourself in the green row.

	How I'm doing on this goal	What I need to adjust or continue working on
Academic Goal		
Reading Goal		
Passion Goal		
Wellness Goal		

ACTIVITIES

My Emotions Chart

Sometimes emotions aren't so easy to understand. You may feel two (or more) emotions at the same time. You may feel a way you have never felt before. Use the following chart to help you understand the emotions you feel as you feel them.

What do you notice about your body (breathing, heart rate, etc)?

What thoughts are going through your mind?

How are your emotions affecting your behavior?

What emotions might you be feeling?

What do you need right now?

Identity Iceberg

Our **identity** is all the parts that makeup who we are inside and out. Some aspects of our identity can be gender, race, ability, religion, culture, language, family, and personality.

Fill in the iceberg below with words that describe you. This chart has some ideas about what you can put in your iceberg.

Top of the Iceberg	What people can see about your identity	Physical attributes, race, gender expression, actions, and behaviors (hobbies or activities), language, etc.
Below the Water	What others may not be able to tell about you at first sight.	Religion/spirituality, family, past places you have lived, skills, personality traits, likes and dislikes, etc.
The Water	Your environment	How you behave in different places and with different people.

MY LEARNING PAST AND FUTURE

Our past experiences at school shape us into the learner we are today. By thinking about our past learning experiences, our struggles, and our successes we can make choices about what kind of learner we want to be this year!

Do your thoughts affect your ability to do your best at school? Explain.

____

____

____

____

____

____

____

Have you had times when you didn't feel like a good student? What happened? Write them on the next page.

Age/Grade	Describe the experience	How I felt as a learner

Sometimes we allow a few small events to change how we feel about ourselves as a learner. What kind of learner do you want to be this year?

Remember, others around you have a learning history too. You often do not have the whole story that has shaped the people, and classmates, around you.

Popping Negative Thoughts

Think through the last few days. What did you say to yourself in your mind? Write them below:

Are your thoughts positive or negative? If they are negative, POP that bubble by placing a big X over it. Now rewrite the thought so it is positive!

Let's practice popping negative thoughts that might come into our mind. Skyler & Royal get back a spelling test with lots of corrections and a low score.

Are your thoughts positive or negative? If they are negative, POP that bubble by placing a big X over it. Now rewrite the thought so it is positive!

Let's practice popping negative thoughts that might come into our mind. Skyler & Royal get back a spelling test with lots of corrections and a low score.

Skyler	Royal
Thought Bubble: "Oh no! I should have practiced more and taken my time on this test." What is Skyler feeling? ______________________________ ______________________________ What will Skyler do? ______________________________ ______________________________ ______________________________ ______________________________	Thought Bubble: "I am the worst speller! I will never be good at spelling." What is Royal feeling? ______________________________ ______________________________ What will Royal do? ______________________________ ______________________________ ______________________________ ______________________________

You get to decide what thoughts to keep and which ones to POP.

Would you Rather: Emotions Edition

Sometimes we do things to make unpleasant emotions last longer. Have you done these things before?

- Try to hide the feeling and not let it show in your face
- Don't recognize the emotion and keep it hidden
- Repeat thoughts in your head and worry, even if the thoughts may be untrue

Let's play Would you Rather. Circle the option you would rather do!

Talk to a trusted adult when you feel anxious	OR	Write about a problem in a journal?
Spend time alone when you're upset	OR	Hang out with your best friend?
Scream into a pillow when you're mad	OR	Squeeze and mold modeling clay?
Take some deep breaths when you're nervous	OR	Spend time outside?
Create art when you need to take a break	OR	Curl up with a good book to read?

You can overcome unpleasant emotions. Did you know that no emotion is bad? You can control how you behave when you feel intense emotions.

Intense Emotions Toolkit

Sometimes we feel such intense, big emotions that we end up acting in a way that hurts ourselves or others.

No emotion is bad. When we behave in a way that hurts ourselves or others because of an emotion, it is best to use a calming tool.

Try the calming tools below and put a ★ next to the ones you want to try next time you feel an intense emotion.

- [ ] Do a kids' yoga video like Cosmic Kids Yoga
- [ ] Use modeling clay to make a monster to express how you're feeling
- [ ] Talk to a trusted adult about how you're feeling
- [ ] Go on a walk or bike ride.
- [ ] Spend time alone in your room doing some deep breathing and relaxing.
- [ ] Listen to your favorite songs.
- [ ] Scream, yell, and stomp your feet far away from other people.
- [ ] Cuddle or play with your pet.
- [ ] Call your grandparent or aunt/uncle to tell them how you're feeling.

What else could you do?

____

Try using one of the ways on this list this week when you feel an unpleasant emotion.

Your Voice is Important

You can use your voice to solve problems, make yourself heard when someone isn't listening, and respond to danger. Read through each scenario below. How might the person's voice have **sounded** in each response?

1. You are at a sleepover and your friend wants to watch a scary movie that you don't think your parents would approve of. You say, "I don't want to watch that movie. Let's pick a different one instead."

____

____

2. You are watching your little brother while your mom went to the grocery store. You're outside playing with a ball when the ball rolls into the street. Your little brother starts to run after it. You say, "Stop!".

____

____

3. You're on the bus when some older kids start picking on your friend. They are getting mean and you say, "Hey, leave them alone."

____

____

When was a time when you used your voice to solve a problem peacefully?

When was a time when you used too big of a voice and were unkind? How could you have calmed down and used your voice differently?

Being Empathetic

Read the following stories. Then put yourself in the other person's shoes and write about what you might be feeling if you were them.

Your friend from camp is coming to your birthday party, but doesn't know any of the other kids that will be at the party.

____

____

____

Your older sister just broke up with her boyfriend.

____

____

____

Your classmate's parents are getting divorced.

____

____

____

Empathy takes practice. You can practice with people you care about and who care about you. Who can you share big feelings with?

Conflict Resolution

Finish the sentences below when having a disagreement. This will help you to be heard, solve the problem, and move forward!

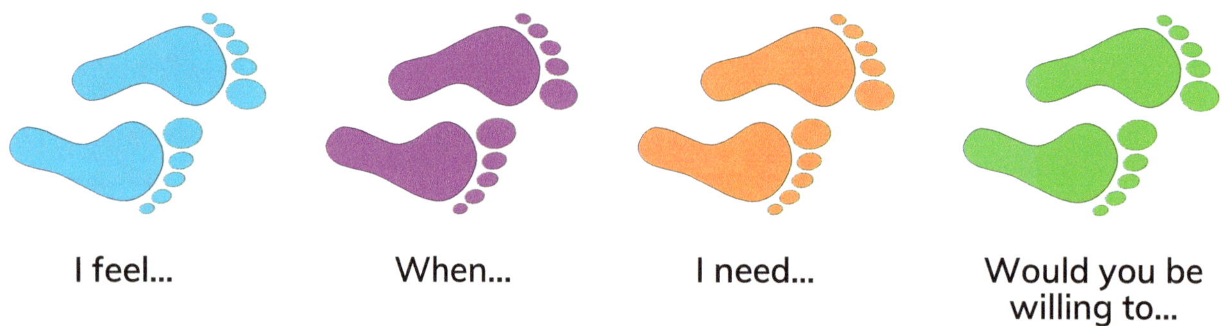

I feel...

When...

I need...

Would you be willing to...

Pick one story below and act it out using the peace path.

1. You lent your special Pokemon card to a friend and they lost it. You are really upset.

2. You're trying to get your work done, but the person next to you keeps trying to talk to you. You're starting to get really frustrated because you can't concentrate.

3. When you get home from a busy day, your mom gives you a list of chores. You feel overwhelmed because you just got home!

4. At the end of practice, your coach takes you aside and says you weren't listening to directions well enough. You think you were listening, but the coach wasn't clear in what they were saying. You feel misunderstood.

5. On the playground, you gather all your friends together, but they can't decide what to play. You just want everyone to get along and have fun together, so you feel upset.

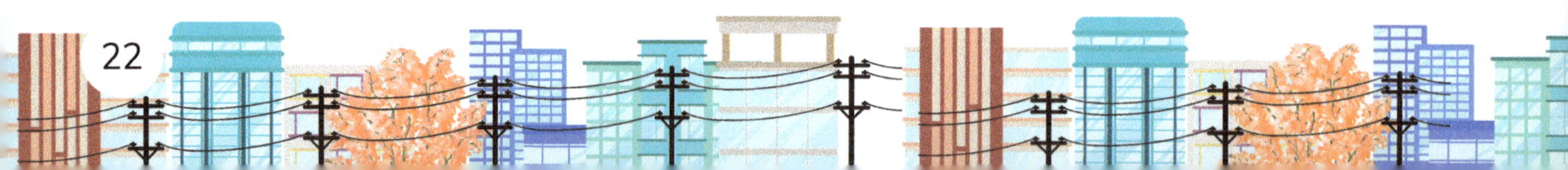

Practice your skit and then perform it. How did your performance go?

____

____

____

____

____

This week, try using the Peace Path at least once when you have a disagreement with someone.

Healthy Friendships

Friendships can be healthy, unhealthy, or sometimes both. What does a healthy friendship look like and what might an unhealthy friendship look like?

Healthy Friendships	Unhealthy Friendships

Sometimes even when we have healthy friendships, our feelings get hurt or we (or our friend) makes mistakes. Read through the following statements and CIRCLE the stories that you're comfortable with in a friendship.

- My friend tells a secret I told them not to tell others about. It has happened 3 times.
- My friend yelled at me because I made a mistake.
- My friend lies to me often.
- My friend says mean things to me to make me feel bad about myself.
- My friend and I sometimes get in fights, but we work them out.

How are you a good friend?

____

____

____

____

____

Setting Personal Boundaries

Think about a time when you set a personal boundary for yourself. What did setting the boundary look and/or sound like? On the next page, draw a comic strip to show what you did to set this boundary. Use thought and word bubbles to show what was thought and said.

When can it be hard to set personal boundaries? How do you feel when people don't respect your boundaries?

____

____

____

____

Can you think of a time when someone set a boundary for you? Did they say "no" or use a different way to show no? (shaking their head, ignoring the question, or another way?) What happened? How did they know the answer was "no" since they didn't say the word "no"?

____

____

____

____

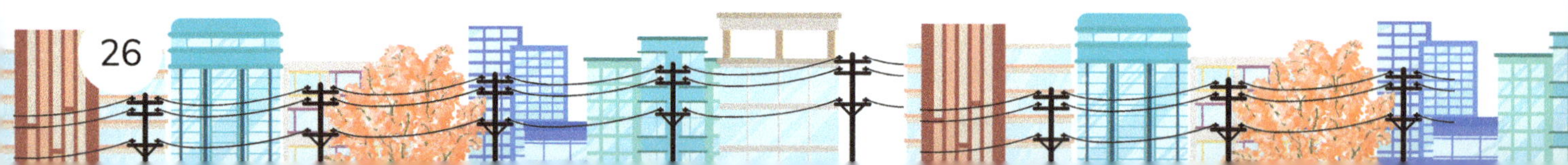

Title: ___________________________________

Empathetic Responses

Empathy is the ability to understand an emotion someone else is feeling even if you have not had the same experience. Empathy takes practice.

Read, or listen to someone read, the book *The Rabbit Listened* by Cori Doerrfeld.

What did the rabbit do to show empathy? ________________________________

____

Read through the following emotions and match it with a way you could show empathy.

A friend is crying.	You listen quietly.
Your mom is stressed out.	You ask if you can give them a hug.
Your teacher is angry.	You ask, "How can I help?"
A classmate is embarrassed.	You ask if they want to talk about it.
Your sibling is worried.	You sit next to them.

How can you show empathy to others?

____

____

____

Being an Upstander

Pretend you are an advice columnist. Read through the story below and give the writer your advice based on what you know about being an upstander and getting help.

Dear Reader,

On the bus ride home I have started noticing a kid in my grade go around and spit on all the bus seats of the younger kids, so when the kids get on the bus they have to sit way back by the window to avoid the spit or sit in it. The bus driver hasn't noticed because this kid is sneaky about how he does it, and the younger kids haven't said anything. Is it my place to do anything? I don't really want to get into a fight with this kid since he could easily start being mean to me too.

Sincerely,
Bus Rider

____

____

____

____

When have you seen someone being an upstander at your school?

____

____

Who are adults who can help you if you need it?

____

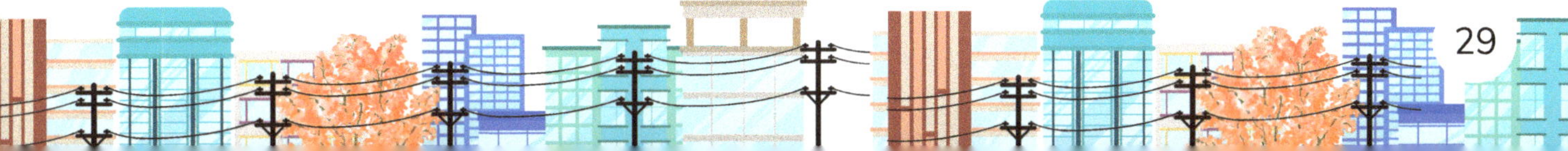

Think before you Speak

Just like toothpaste, we can't take our words and thoughts back. Before you speak to others and before you think thoughts to yourself, remember to THINK.

Is it True?
Is it Helpful?
Is it Inspiring?
Is it Necessary?
Is it Kind?

Describe a time when you wanted to say something that didn't follow THINK. Why did you decide to stay silent?

Did staying silent help your relationship with that person (or build yourself up)? How?

What are some tools you can use to determine whether you should speak up, stay silent, or pop a negative thought bubble?

My Power of Words Toolkit

- ______________________________
- ______________________________
- ______________________________
- ______________________________

IF THIS...THEN THAT

Including other people doesn't just mean saying yes when others ask if they can join you in play. It means being aware of other people being excluded.

Let's practice with the game If This...Then That. Read the "If" words and then finish the sentence by writing "then". The first one has been done for you.

1. If the same student is always left out when playing at recess, then they may feel lonely and excluded.

2. If the same student is always picked last when picking teams in gym, then

____

3. If you're talking about a birthday party you and your friends attended but one friend is staying silent, then

____

4. If a kid asks to join in playing and they say no and then asks your group to play, then

____

5. If a new person stands near your friend group but doesn't join in the conversation, then

____

You can notice when others feel excluded even if they don't say anything. Include others and be kind.

A Poem about Caring

"In Lak'ech" is a simple poem of only 6 lines, but it is very meaningful. Brainstorm ways that you can take care of yourself and the people around you.

1 ____

____

2 ____

____

3 ____

____

4 ____

____

5 ____

____

6 ____

____

Now try writing your own poem using the ways you brainstormed above. You can use each of your brainstormed ideas for one line of your poem or mix all your ideas together. Your poem should be short and only 6 lines long.

Title: ____

Understanding Others

What does it mean to be understanding?

Think about 3 different people that you find hard to understand at times. Then think of ways you can understand them better. We've done an example for you!

Person	How I can Understand them Better
My Grandma	*I don't talk to her much, just the two of us. I should spend time talking to her to learn more about her life.*

Now try to put your plans into action so you can better understand some of the people in your life.

Learning Respect

You have role models who show you respect and show you *how* to be respectful. Think about one person in your life who really shows respect. Then fill in the activity below to remember all the ways they model respect to you and others.

Name: ______________________________

Things they SAY to show respect:

____

____

____

Ways they show respect with their ACTIONS:

____

____

____

Ways they BEHAVE to show respect:

____

____

____

I'M PART OF A COMMUNITY

You are part of many communities -- a family, a school, a neighborhood, and maybe a team. When you become part of a community, you learn to stay true to yourself and also care for people who are different from you.

Think about some of your favorite songs and pick a song for each community you belong to. The song will be different for each community, since all groups feel, sound, and look a bit different.

Here is an example:

Community: Art Club

Song: "Try Everything" by Shakira

Reason: I just joined art club because I love art. I'm excited to try something new and meet more people who also love art.

Sometimes people mistreat others based on differences. Be an upstander and understand that differences make us stronger!

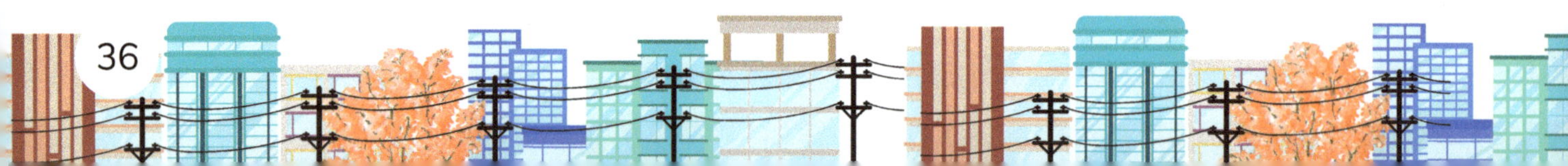

Community: ____________________ Song: Reason:	Community: ____________________ Song: Reason:
Community: ____________________ Song: Reason:	Community: ____________________ Song: Reason:
Community: ____________________ Song: Reason:	Community: ____________________ Song: Reason:

We Need Mirrors and Windows

A **MIRROR** experience is where we see lots of similarities between ourselves and others.

A **WINDOW** experience are where we learn about people who are different from us.

Let's play BINGO. To play, you must get three in a row. Read through each box and put an X through it if you can answer the question based on a book you have read before. You cannot use a book more than once!

Can you tell which boxes are about mirror books and which ones are about window books? Color the mirror book boxes green and the window book boxes blue!

A book where the main character was really similar to me! Title: ____________________ Name of the character: ____________________	A book where the action took place in a different country. Title: ____________________ Country in the book: ____________________	A book where I learned something new. Title: ____________________ What I learned: ____________________ ____________________
A book that made me feel curious to learn more. Title: ____________________ What I want to learn about: ____________________	A book that made me feel really good about myself. Title: ____________________ What made me feel so good: ____________________	A book where the main character was really different from me! Title: ____________________ Name of the character: ____________________
A book that was set in a different time period. Title: ____________________ Time period: ____________________	A book where the character was like me but also different. Title: ____________________ Name of the character: ____________________	A book where the family structure was different from mine. Title: ____________________ Family Differences: ____________________

Disagreeing Respectfully

Think about 3 different disagreements you have had. Then write down what you disagreed about and write an I Statement with how you *could* have disagreed respectfully.

Disagreement: ____

____

I Statement: ____

____

Disagreement: ____

____

I Statement: ____

____

Disagreement: ____

____

I Statement: ____

____

When you use an I Statement, it doesn't mean you will win the argument. Instead it is a way to share your thoughts and feelings in a respectful way.

BE AUTHENTIC

"Fitting in is becoming who you need to be accepted. Belonging is being your authentic self and knowing that no matter what happens, you belong to you."

- Brene Brown

What does this quotation mean to you and about friendships?

____

____

Has anyone ever said they hate something you liked, and you pretended to agree with them? Why do we do this?

____

____

____

How can you belong instead of just fitting in?

____

____

____

Do you think your friendships are healthy? Or are there some friendships that may not be very healthy? What can you do to change this so all your friendships are healthy?

____

____

____

WORKING TOGETHER

You can work with other people to collaborate, make decisions, and create something new!

Practice collaborating by picking a game below and playing it with a group of friends or your family

Collaborative Games to try:

- Dragon Dash
- Race to the Treasure
- Hoot Owl Hoot
- OutFoxed!
- Gnomes at Night
- Code Names
- Cauldron Quest

What makes collaboration hard? What can you do about it?

____

____

____

____

____

You've Got a Friend

Sometimes we need help and other times we can be helpful to others. Listen to the song "You've Got a Friend" by James Taylor.

What thought stuck out to you when you were listening to the song?

____

____

Who are the people in your life that you can ask for help from?

A trusted adult ____

A friend ____

A teacher or coach _____________________________________

Other: ____

How do you help people in your community?

____

____

Take time this week to be helpful in your community and notice where there are places that need your help.

Modeling Safety

It is important to keep yourself safe and model ways to keep your body safe, feelings safe, and stay safe online. Work with a small group to create a safety booklet, then share your booklet with younger students.

Your booklet should include:

- A title page showing the topic you are covering -- safety
- A page on keeping your body safe
- A page on keeping your feelings safe
- A page on how you can stay safe online

Create your safety booklet by taking a new piece of paper and folding it in half so you have 4 "pages".

Once you're done with your safety booklet, decide who you will share this information with, and when.

____

____

____

Kindness Cards

One thoughtful way to show kindness is to send kind cards to people you care about and people you want to give a compliment to.

This week, write 5 kindness cards by telling the person how much they mean to you, giving them a compliment, or saying thank you.

Who will you write a Kindness Card for this week?

1. ______________________________

2. ______________________________

3. ______________________________

4. ______________________________

5. ______________________________

How does it feel after giving out your five Kindness Cards?

____

____

____

____

Be Mindful

Our brains have two parts: the downstairs brain and the upstairs brain.

Upstairs Brain	Decisions we make for ourselves (example: solving problems, being creative, our behavior, and more!)	
Downstairs Brain	Decisions are made for us (example: beating of your heart, breathing, big emotions, and more!)	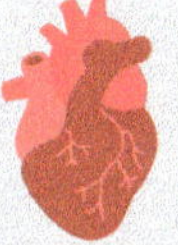 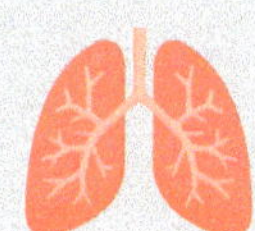

Can you think of decisions you have made with your downstairs brain that you can then use your upstairs brain to solve instead? You can think of things that have happened in the past that you wish you had used your upstairs brain, or examples where you did use your upstairs brain.

Downstairs Brain	Upstairs Brain
You feel really sad.	*You decide to talk to a trusted adult about why you are so sad.*

We can connect our upstairs brain and downstairs brain using mindful breathing. Try it by slowly breathing in deeply and then slowly breathing out again. Do this 5 times and notice how your mind and body relax.

Learning from Mistakes

All people make mistakes. Mistakes can help us learn. When we make a mistake, talk to yourself like a friend and pop your negative thought bubbles. What are some things you can tell yourself when you make a mistake?

- ________________________________
- ________________________________
- ________________________________
- ________________________________

Draw a picture of a time you made a mistake, but learned from it.

The next time you make a mistake, what do you want to do?

____

____

INQUISITIVE

Inquisitive is a big word that simply means being curious. Are you inquisitive?

Being inquisitive is a great way to be flexible with your thinking, stay open-minded, and keep learning and growing!

Pick one of the activities below where you can be inquisitive this week, then do it. Report back on how it went in the reflection.

Activities:

- Bake a cake with a trusted adult. Learn what the different ingredients do to make the cake taste, look, and feel spongy and soft.
- Go to the library and check out several picture books on a topic you don't know much about. Read the books.
- Look up a video on the Internet (with a trusted adult) on how something is made. Learn about how it was made or created.

What was the most fun part of being inquisitive with the activity you picked?

____

____

____

What was the most challenging part of this activity?

____

____

____

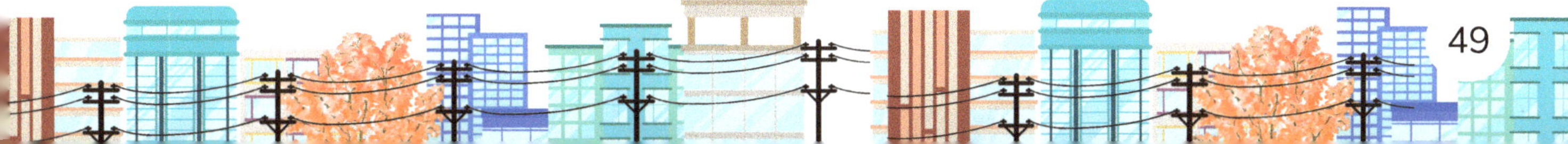

Balancing Your Life

Technology is really helpful: you can relax while watching TV or playing video games, learn new things from learning videos, and listen to music that motivates you all using technology. But technology can also be harmful if you use it too much.

Can you give advice to the following kids for how to balance their life without taking out their favorite things?

Jose loves to watch movies. After school he sits on his couch and watches movies for several hours.

What advice would you give Jose to help him balance his life better?

____

____

Amanda plays video games all weekend. Sometimes she meets up with friends online to play together, but they don't get together in person.

What advice would you give Amanda to help her balance her life better?

____

____

Alex is a perfectionist and wants only the highest grades. He gets upset if he doesn't get all the questions right on his tests and homework. He spends hours doing homework each night.

What advice would you give Alex to help him balance his life better?

____

____

What do you do too much of? How can you be more balanced?

____

____

____

____

YOU CAN CHANGE THE WORLD!

What are your strengths?

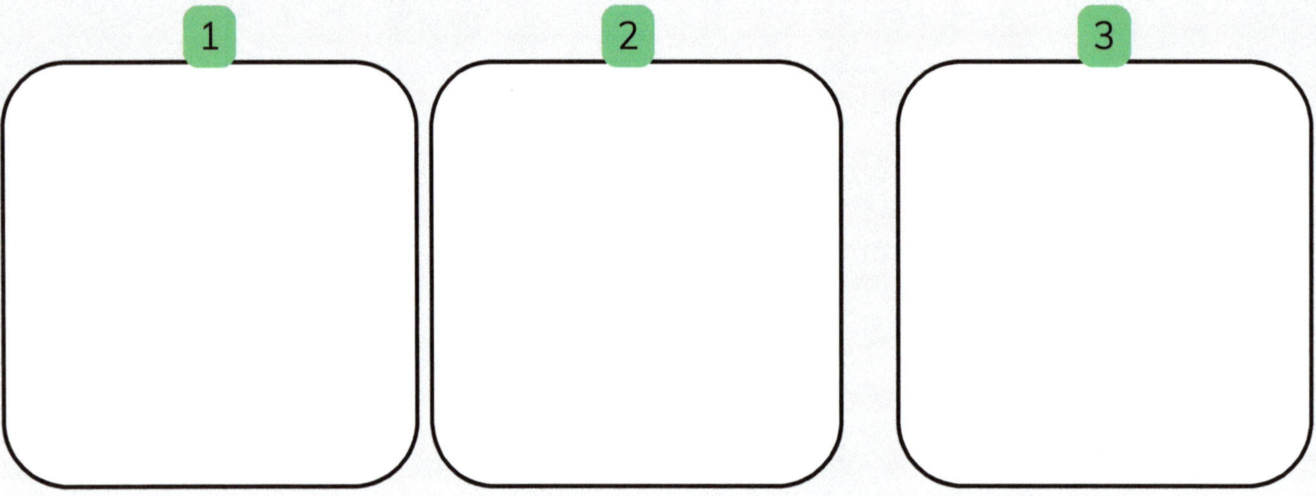

Share your strengths with a small group in class. Together make a list of 3 ways you can use your strengths together to create a better world.

1. ______________________________

____

2. ______________________________

3. ______________________________

____

You are never too young to make a change, get out of your comfort zone, and try something new! Look through your list with your whole class and together decide on one way you all can work together this week to create a better world. Write your plan below.

What we will do:	
When we will do it:	
How we will do it:	

Being Responsible

You are not responsible for others, but you are responsible for how your actions and words affect others.

Read through the following sentences. Can you determine which ones you are responsible for and which ones you are not responsible for?

You are in a bad mood and yell at your mom.

I'm responsible.   I'm not responsible.

Your younger brother is sad and crying.

I'm responsible.   I'm not responsible.

You can't find the garbage can, so just throw your wrapper on the ground.

I'm responsible.   I'm not responsible.

You decide not to do your homework for today.

I'm responsible.   I'm not responsible.

Your friend asks you to do something you're not comfortable doing, so you say no. They are disappointed.

I'm responsible.   I'm not responsible.

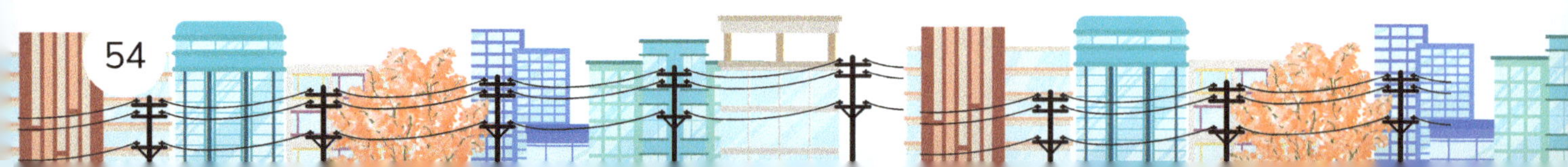

Being a Leader

Leaders are strong not only because they like to lead and are confident in themselves, but also because they have people who support them and they are resilient.

Fill in the spaces below with your answers to see how you can be a strong leader in your community.

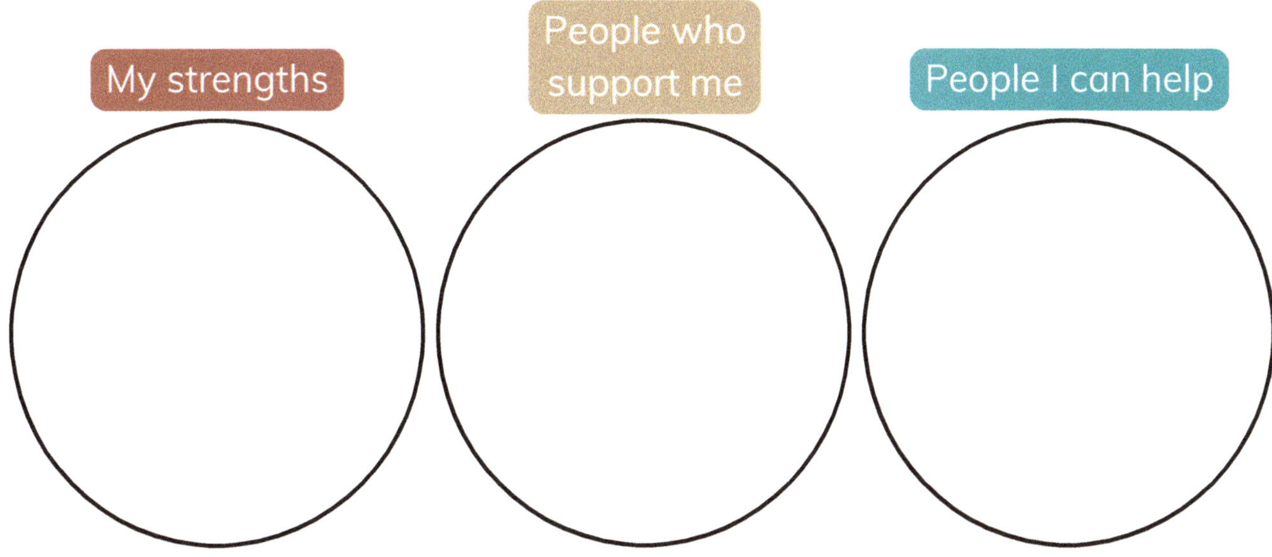

Resilience in leaders means that even when a leader encounters a problem or challenge, they can cope. Coping may mean talking through the problem with someone they trust, pushing through even when it's uncomfortable, taking a break, or changing a plan.

Describe a time when you have been resilient.

___

___

___

___

Noticing a Growth Mindset

Your mind is powerful! When you tell yourself positive, encouraging thoughts -- you end up doing better! You are using a growth mindset!

Practice by using your classroom library or neighborhood library. Find picture books where one of the characters uses a growth mindset. We've given you an example.

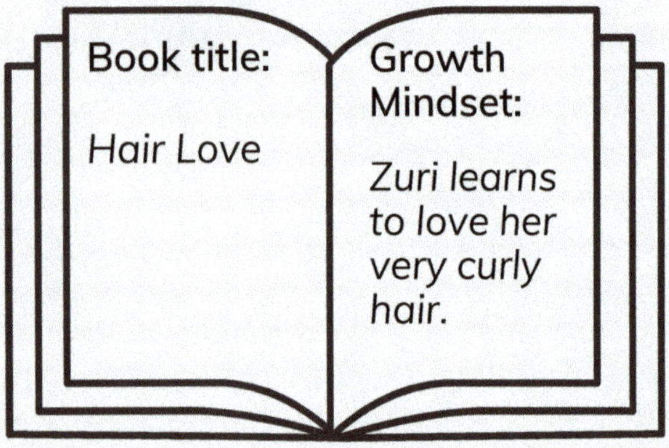

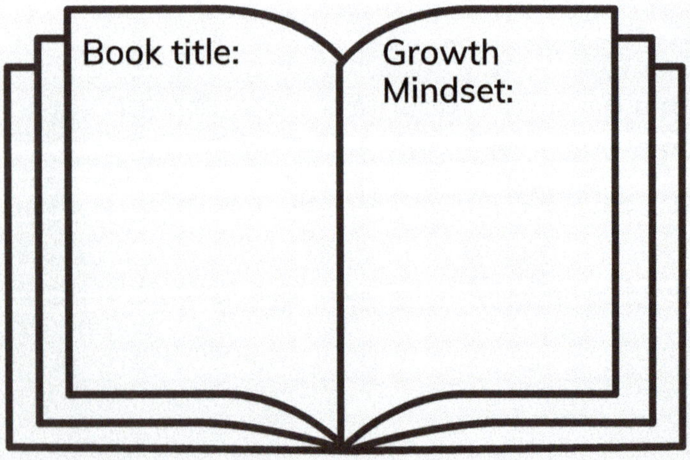

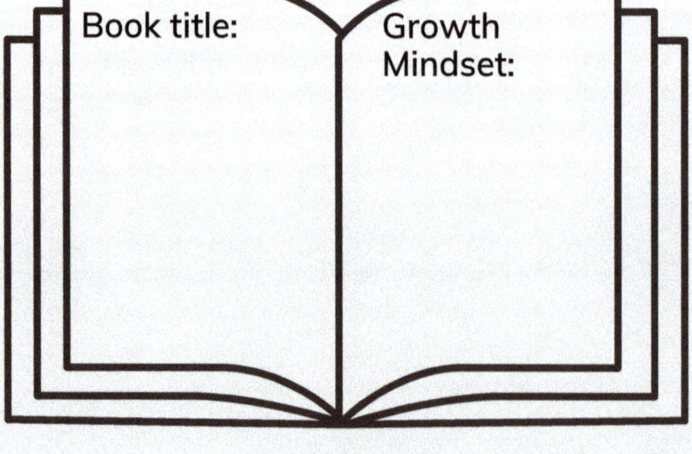

Book title:

Hair Love

Growth Mindset:

Zuri learns to love her very curly hair.

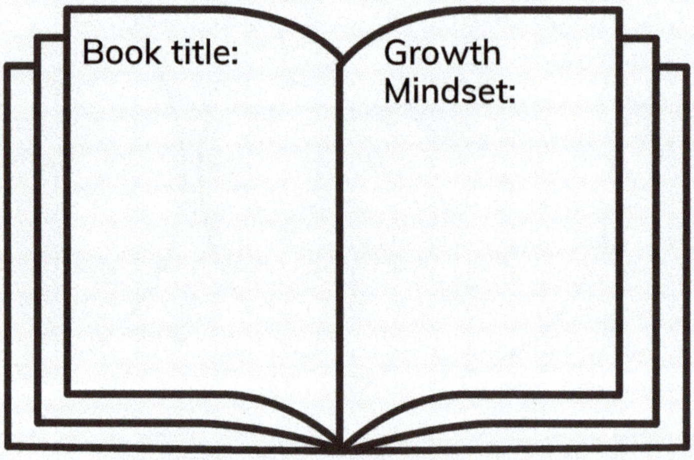

Book title:

Growth Mindset:

Book title:

Growth Mindset:

Book title:

Growth Mindset:

You Can Do It!

When life gets hard, do you give up or keep on going? If you keep going, even if you're struggling, that's called resilience. If you sometimes give up too easily, you can use positive affirmations to encourage yourself to keep going.

Fill in the bubbles below with positive affirmations you can tell yourself next time you are struggling. For example: I can do hard things.

Wants versus Needs

Staying organized can be hard, but one way you can get better at organizing your life is by determining what you *want* to do versus what you *need* to do.

For example, you may *want* to watch TV, but you know you *need* to do your homework. You can organize your day responsibly by first doing your homework and then watching some TV.

Write down one *want* and one *need* on two separate slips of paper. After your teacher collects them, see if you and your group can identify all the slips of paper into the want category and the need category.

How can understanding your *wants* versus your *needs* help you stay organized?

____

____

____

____

____

Respecting No

It can be hard when we hear 'no.' When we get a no, we need to look at the person and say OK. It is important to stay calm in the moment. If we disagree with the answer, we can talk about it at another time, but we should not argue about it right away.

Usually, there is a reason why a person has answered no. Most people don't want to keep talking about it. No means no and we need to move on.

Gather in a large group. Make a circle so you can all see each other's faces. Then use the discussion questions below to reflect on respecting a "no".

Discussion Questions:

How does your body feel when you first hear the word "no"?

What do you usually THINK when you first hear the word "no"?

Are there times when it is easier to accept a no answer? What makes it easier?

Describe a time when you heard "no" and it was really hard, but you stayed calm and respected their decision?

You Are Your Own Best Friend

It is important to use positive self-talk. In small groups, practice and then act out one story where you use a positive self-talk, or growth mindset, sentence.

Your soccer team has been winning almost all your games. As a team, you all have been working really hard and during practice you are all really focused. Today you are playing a team that isn't ranked as high as your team, but they are ahead of you in points right at the beginning of the match. You line up to kick the ball into the goal and end up missing. In front of the whole team and all the fans!

There is a special program at school for kids interested in coding. In the class, you get pulled for part of your regular class's math class so you can participate in this coding program. But in order to get in, you have to have a high test score. You are taking the test today to see if you can get in, but you're so nervous that your hands are shaking.

There is a new kid at school and your best friend and the new kid are neighbors! Your best friend introduces you to the new kid and you are friendly, but then realize your best friend has already spent the whole weekend with this new kid after telling you that they couldn't hang out because they already had plans. You start feeling jealous. Are you about to lose your best friend?

Your thoughts are powerful. What thoughts can keep you positive even when things are difficult?

____

____

 ____

Personal Space

Personal space is the space that is right next to your body. Some people like to have a lot of space around them without other people too close to them. Other people don't mind having less personal space, or even being touched by others.

Here are some important things to notice about personal space:

1. Pay attention to how close your body is to the personal space of other people.
2. Pay attention to how other people react when you are close to them or touch them.
3. If someone is in your personal space and you don't like it, use your words to tell them how you feel. You could say, "I don't like it when you're in my personal space, please back up." or "I feel uncomfortable when you're in my personal space, please back up."

Let's practice. What would you say in each of these stories?

You walk into your friend's house and her younger sister runs up to you and gives you a hug. You need more personal space.

You may say: ______________________________

____

____

My Circle of Control

Brainstorm things you can and can't control in your life (at home, at school, with friends, with family, and your feelings and behaviors). Then place those things either **INSIDE** the circle if you can control it or **OUTSIDE** the circle if you can't control it.

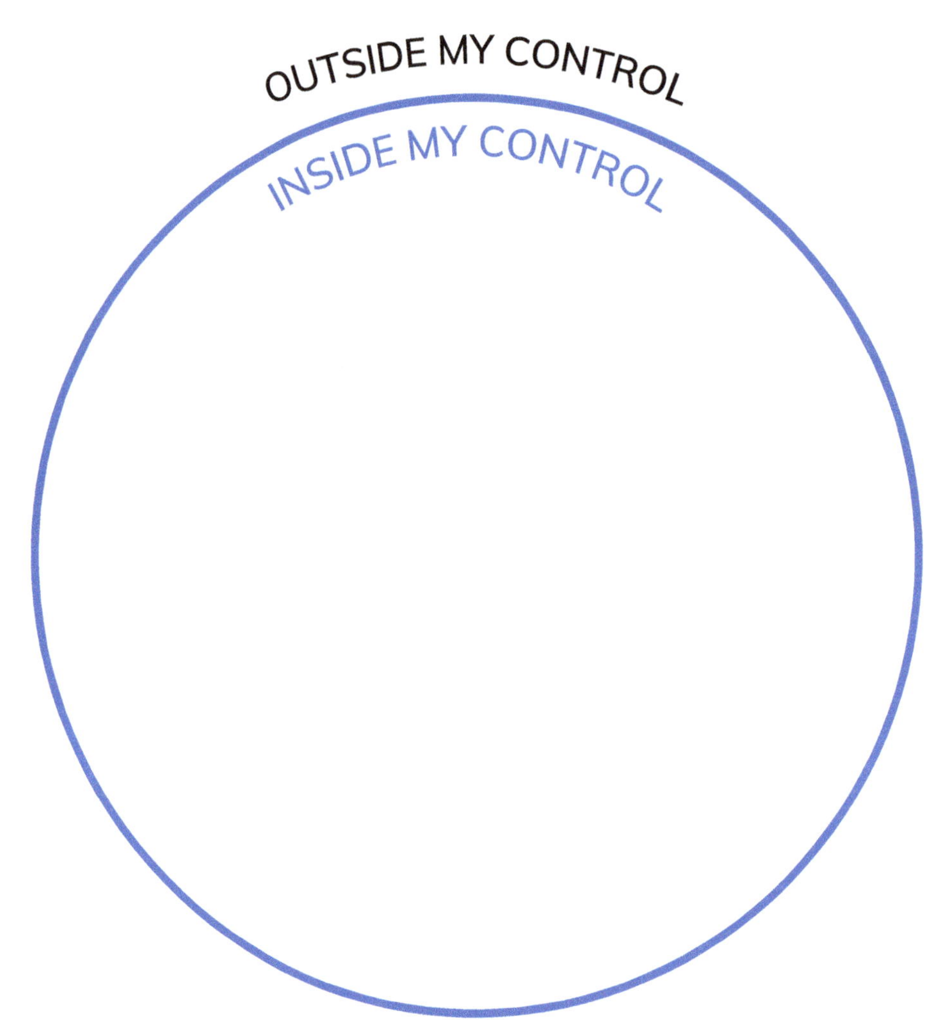

Remember, if you can't control something, you can let go of the stress and worry. How can you let go of the things you can't control?

____

____

____

You and your friends are playing tag on the playground. You get tagged but instead of the friend tagging you and then running away, they stay close to you -- too close. You feel uncomfortable because they are in your personal space.

You may say: ____

____

____

Your grandma comes to visit your house and gives you a hug. After the hug she wants to sit on the sofa with you and cuddle, but you don't feel comfortable cuddling that close right now. You wanted a hug and now want to play a game at the table. You need more personal space right now.

You may say: ____

____

____

Seeking Help

Have you ever done the following?

- You need help, but you feel embarrassed so stay silent.
- You are confused, but decide to just go ahead with what you think you should do because you don't want to bother the other person.
- You ask for help and the person says "yes, wait five minutes" but you don't want to wait, so you just go ahead and try without the help.
- You raise your hand to get help, but then the discussion ends and there isn't time to ask for help anymore.

Can you think of other times when you have wanted to ask for help, but haven't? Write it below.

- ____

  ____
- ____

  ____

This type of thing happens to everyone, but it's important to be confident in yourself and get the help you need.

Journal below on what you will do next time when you need help, but hesitate to ask or wait for help.

My Journal:

____

____

____

____

____

____

____

____

____

____

____

____

____

The Art of Apologizing

It can be really hard to apologize and say you're sorry. Some grown-ups even have trouble apologizing.

It's important to learn to apologize when you have done something wrong. When you say you're sorry, it's important to not just say "I'm sorry" and move on, but to apologize and make a plan for moving forward.

Here are some things you can include in your apology.

"I'm sorry for..." (say what you did that was wrong)

"It was wrong because..." (why were your actions hurtful)

"What can I do to make it better?"

"Next time I will..."

When someone apologizes to you, you need to look the person in the eye and listen to what they are saying. You can help them come up with ideas to fix the problem. Finally, you can accept the apology in many ways. Some ideas of what you could say are:

- "I accept your apology"
- "I forgive you"
- "Thank you for telling me"
- "We are still friends"

Read the story below. Underline the part in the story where the person apologizes. Highlight the part in the story where the person accepts the apology. ~~Cross out~~ any parts of the apology that are not helpful.

Your friend loaned you a book because you both have been reading the *Wings of Fire* series but you don't have book 5 in the series yet. Unfortunately as you are reading one evening, you rip a page as you are turning it. You know your friend bought these books with their own money and you feel really bad.

In the morning, you see your friend at school. You ask to talk to them alone and say, "I'm so sorry. I was reading the book last night and accidentally ripped a page. I feel really bad because I know how important the book is to you, although the pages are really thin so it made it easy for it to rip. I put some clear tape over the rip, but is there something else I can do to make this better?"

Your friend says, "Thanks for telling me. It's okay. The clear tape works and it looks like the rip wasn't through the whole page. I can still read the page."

Practice Compromising

Compromising means to come to an agreement that doesn't give everyone exactly what they want, but works for the group as a whole.

For example, you and your friend are trying to decide what game to play. You want to play tag but your friend wants to play soccer. You compromise and decide to create an obstacle course on the playground instead since that's something you both are willing to do.

There are lots of different ways to compromise. Can you think of how you can find a good compromise when you run into problems?

- ____
  ____
- ____
  ____
- ____
  ____

Sometimes we *think* we are compromising, when we aren't. Can you tell the difference? Read the stories determine whether a fair compromise was made.

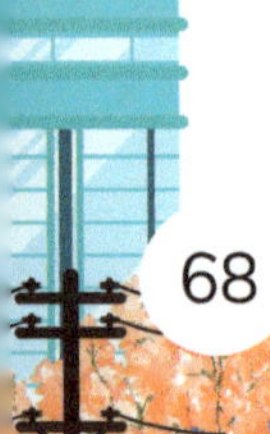

As a class you can decide on your field trip: the zoo or the aquarium, but not both. Your teacher takes a vote and it's almost split evenly on where your class wants to go. You talk together and decide you will go to the zoo on the field trip, but then in your next science unit you will learn about sea creatures and visit an aquarium online through an e-experience. You and your classmates feel happy with this decision.

This was a good compromise   This was not a compromise

You and your siblings are going to play together on a rainy day. You want to build a big Lego city, but your sibling wants to do an indoor scavenger hunt. You tell your sibling that a scavenger hunt is too hard and to come play Legos with you. You play together, but you can tell your sibling is disappointed the whole time.

This was a good compromise   This was not a compromise

You and your friend are riding your bikes. You want to ride through a rough trail in the woods because it's more exciting, but your friend wants to ride on the boring sidewalk. You talk through why each of you wants to go a different way and you learn your friend is scared to go on the trail. You decide you will go on the sidewalk and ride to the bike park where there are some fun ramps to go up and down. You both feel good about this decision.

This was a good compromise   This was not a compromise

Your mom cooked dinner, but you hate what she made. She asks you to eat with the family and tells you she isn't going to make you a different meal. You ask if you could make yourself a sandwich and promise to clean up afterwards and sit with the family to eat. She agrees. You both feel good about this decision.

This was a good compromise   This was not a compromise

Staying Flexible

If you have a flexible body, it's probably because you train your body to stretch and slowly over time you have gotten more and more flexible.

To have a flexible mind, you also need to train and practice so you can become more and more flexible.

Let's look at an example. In which story were you a flexible thinker?

1 You get a new chemistry kit for your birthday and want to make a solution that is teal (your favorite color), but the direction booklet doesn't have instructions for making anything teal. You feel frustrated and ask your mom for help.

2 You get a new chemistry kit for your birthday and want to make a solution that is teal (your favorite color), but the direction booklet doesn't have instructions for making anything teal. So you start experimenting with different color tablets and stirring different amounts of water into a few different test tubes until you get the color you want.

Describe a time when you were flexible in your thinking. What happened? Write about it below or share it with a partner.

STAYING HEALTHY

There are so many parts of us that we need to keep healthy:

1. our mind
2. our emotions
3. our heart
4. our body

For this lesson, we will focus on keeping our bodies healthy. We can keep our bodies healthy by moving and not doing the same activity all the time. For instance, if you've been sitting at your desk for a long time or watching TV for a long time, you need to get up and move your body to stay healthy.

Practice by creating your own Movement Plan. In each of the squares pick an activity, then pick how many times you will do this movement. The first one has been done for you.

When you have been sitting for too long and need to get up to move your body, pull out your Movement Plan and do all 6 actions to get your body moving!

My Movement Plan

Jumping Jacks 5 times		

Healthy Decisions

You can keep a healthy mind, body, and heart by making healthy decisions. Use the chart below to think of ways you keep your mind, body, and heart healthy. Use the intersection of the circles to put things that keep two or all three of these things healthy.

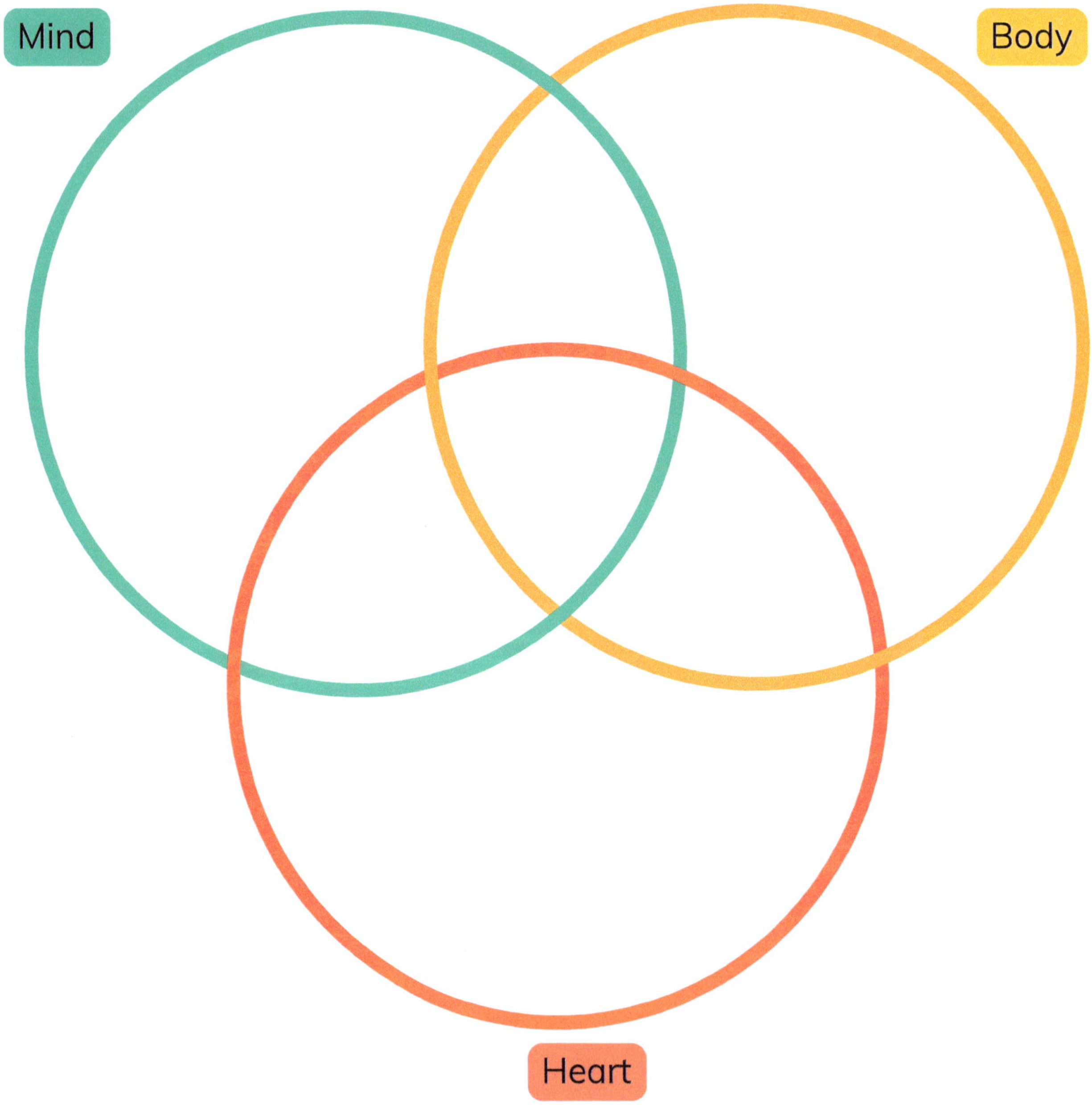

Mind

Body

Heart

Make a goal to give each part of yourself some love and attention.

A MIND goal: ______________________________

____

____

A BODY goal: ______________________________

____

____

A HEART goal: ______________________________

____

____

Challenge Yourself!

How do you feel when you try something new? Circle all the emotions you feel when you try something new:

Scared	Nervous	Confident
Excited	Uncertain	Determined

When you try new things, you can learn more about yourself. It's okay to challenge yourself. When you challenge yourself, you may want to take small steps to get yourself comfortable.

For example: You are scared to sing on stage for your music performance so you first try singing at home in front of a mirror, then sing in front of your family, then in front of your friends, and now you're ready to sing for your performance!

What is something you want to challenge yourself to do?

____

Now break your challenge into smaller steps like the example above.

1. ____

2. ____

3. ____

4. ____

5. ____

Use the steps you created to try something new!

How did it go? Talk with a group of friends or your classmates on how it went!

Gratitude Journal

When we take a few moments to reflect on things we are grateful for we create a healthier well-being in our mind, body, and heart. One way to create a gratitude practice is to create a gratitude journal where every day you write down one thing you are thankful for and why you are thankful for this person, thing, event, feeling, etc. Try it below!

My Gratitude Journal

Discussion Questions

What makes you special?

What is a feeling that helps you feel strong and happy? When do you feel this emotion the most?

If you were trapped on a deserted island, what is the one thing you would want with you? Why?

If you could invent anything, what would it be?

If you could have any super power, what would it be? Why?

What do you do when you are stressed out?

What is the hardest part of every day life for you?

What is a goal you have for yourself?

Describe a time when you were courageous and brave. What happened? How did you feel?

Describe a time when you got through a difficult time. What happened?

If you could meet any famous person (from now or in the past), who would you want to meet? Why?

How could you be a better friend?

If you could spend the whole day with your friend doing anything, what would you do?

When have you stood up for someone else? What did you say? What happened?

What do you do when someone asks you for help? How do you feel?

How do you think kids learn to be kind?

Is it better to be overly confident or not confident enough? Explain.

Why is it important to understand other people's emotions?

What do you say or what do you do to help others be included in group activities?

Think of someone special in your life. What are their greatest strengths?

How do you know what you hear or read is the truth?

Why is it important to share your thoughts and opinions with others?

What is your favorite sport or activity to do to move your body and keep you healthy?

What is your favorite activity or hobby to keep your mind and heart healthy?

Describe a time when there was a consequence because of something you did. What happened?

Projects

STUDENT ACTIVISM

For this project, take some time to research historical and current activists working toward environmental and social justice. Then create a work of art to display your research and promote change.

There are plenty of Student Activists to inspire you as well. Display your research with a short write up and a work of art turning them into a comic book style super hero for the people and the plant!

1. Research

An activist simply means a person who is doing something to create change in their community or the world.

For example, Greta Thunberg is a young woman encouraging countries to lower carbon emissions to better our planet's climate.

Use the form below to do your own research.

The issue / topic	What I learned
________________	____________________________________
	____________________________________
	____________________________________
	____________________________________
	____________________________________
	____________________________________

1. Research

The issue / topic

What I learned

2. Creation

Pick one issue you researched to focus on for this project.

You will now create a piece of art promoting your issue. Your piece of art could be:

- a graphic novel with a super hero
- a poster
- a digital collage

Before you decide what to create, take a look at some examples at https://amplifier.org/education/

3. Reflect

What did you learn throughout this project?

____

____

____

____

How will what you learned change your actions in the future?

____

____

____

____

A Window Read-a-thon

You and your class are challenged to a Read-a-Thon over the next month of school by reading window books.

How many books can you read over the next 30 days that show diverse experiences, cultures, and places?

A Read-a-Thon is simply a reading challenge.

In this challenge, you need to read as many WINDOW books as possible. You can pick novels, poetry, short stories, non-fiction, and even picture books! As long as the book is a window book for you, it counts!

Fill out the activity below to organize yourself and get ready for the Read-a-Thon!

Our class Read-a-Thon will take place

from ______________________ to ______________________.

My goal is to read __________ books!

Remember, a **window** book is a book that focuses on a experience that is new to you. Perhaps a different time place, or the book is placed in a different country, or the main character has a very different lived experience than you.

BOOKS I READ

Book Title	This book was a window for me because...
1	____
	____
2	____
	____
3	____
	____
4	____
	____
5	____
	____
6	____
	____
7	____
	____

I read __________ books!

As a class, we read __________ books!

What was your favorite book? Why?

____

____

____

What did you learn about yourself by reading these window books?

____

____

____

What did you learn about other experiences by reading these window books?

____

____

____

Being a Helping Hand

You don't have to be a grown-up to help others. Helping other people is one way you can show gratitude, grow your own well-being, and lift others up.

This month, use the calendar below to focus on ways you can help others. Once you have completed an activity, shade it or cross it out. We left a few spaces blank so you can fill in other ways you have been helpful.

Can you do all the activities within one month?

Help a friend on the playground.	Clean your room.	Volunteer by picking up liter in your school.	Take care of your pet.	Help with cooking dinner.
Help your teacher with a task.	Call an elderly family member to say hi and chat.	Carry something for someone else.	Set the table or do the dishes.	Clean up liter outside.
Take out the trash.	Tend to a garden or potted plant.	Help a classmate with their homework.	Volunteer at an animal shelter or food packing group.	Create cheerful cards to give to the local nursing home.
Bake cookies & deliver them to First Responders.	Create a few blessing bags to hand out.	Donate gently used clothes to a charity.		

Resources

READ A BOOK!

Here are some can't-put-down books. Use the chart to select the best book for you (and remember you can find these books at your local library, so you don't have to buy the book!).

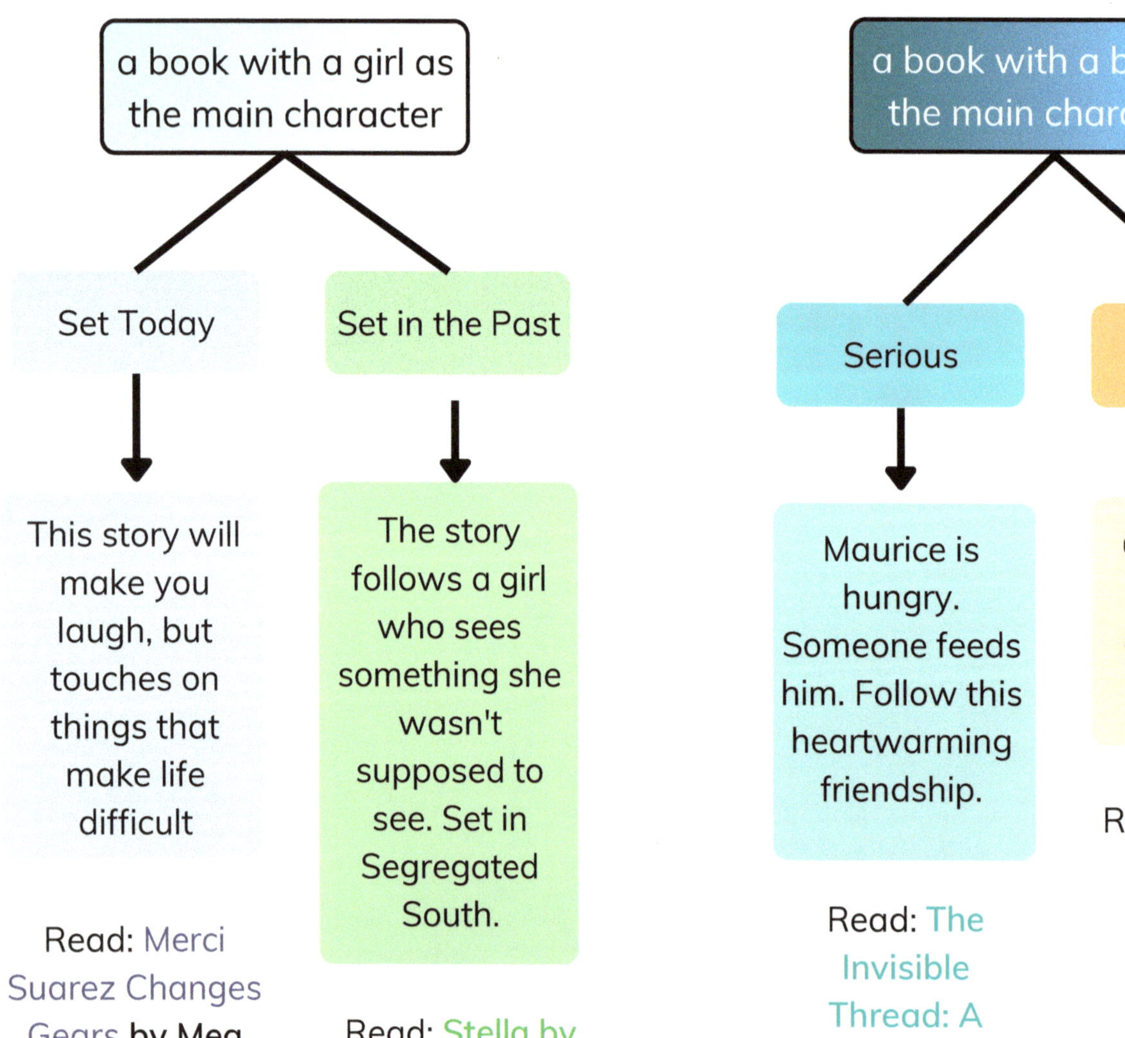

My Book Journal

Track the books you have read on the chart below.

Title	Author	Rate the Book
		☆☆☆☆☆
		☆☆☆☆☆
		☆☆☆☆☆
		☆☆☆☆☆
		☆☆☆☆☆
		☆☆☆☆☆
		☆☆☆☆☆
		☆☆☆☆☆

Wellbeing Tooklit

Pick one of the tools below when you are feeling an intense emotion, need to calm down, or want to take a break from a busy life.

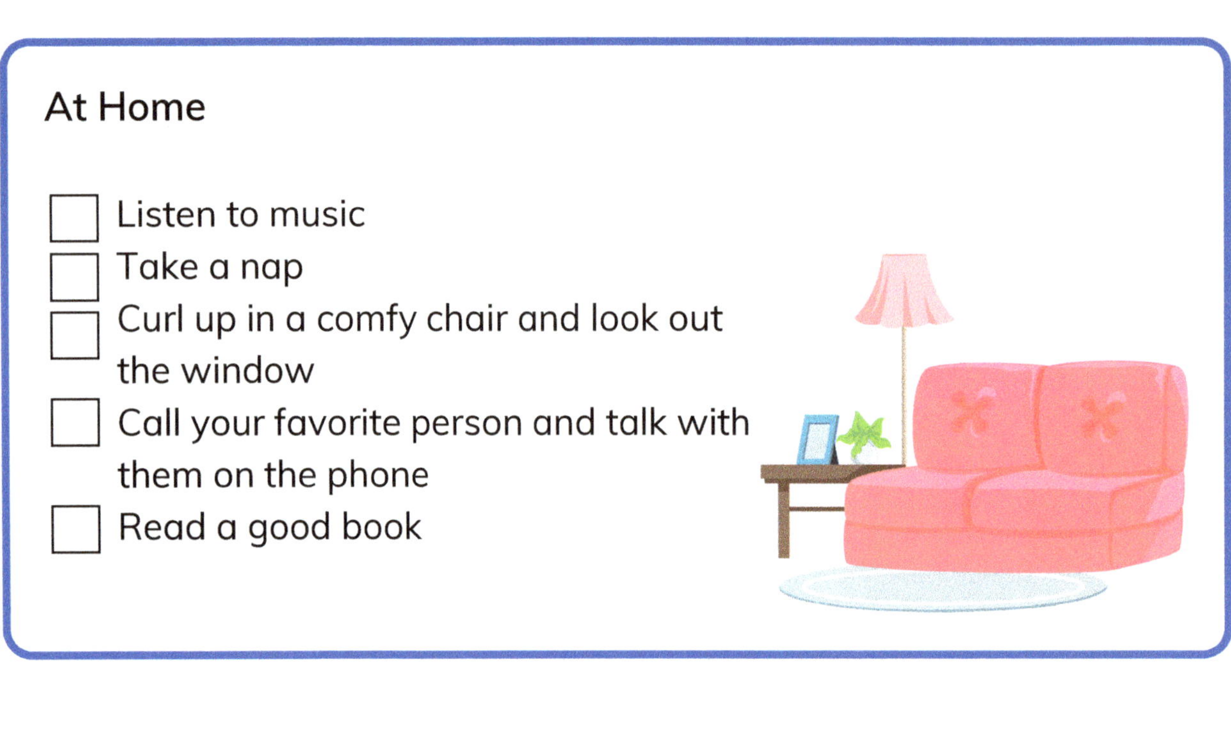

At Home

- [ ] Listen to music
- [ ] Take a nap
- [ ] Curl up in a comfy chair and look out the window
- [ ] Call your favorite person and talk with them on the phone
- [ ] Read a good book

Outside

- [ ] Go for a walk
- [ ] Ride your bike
- [ ] Sit and listen to the sounds you hear
- [ ] Watch the clouds and think about what animals each cloud looks like
- [ ] Collect leaves and notice their differences

Anywhere

- [ ] Sit and take some deep breaths
- [ ] Close your eyes and count to 10
- [ ] Imagine your favorite place; go there in your mind
- [ ] Stop and listen to the sounds around you. Can you find 10 unique sounds?
- [ ] Move your body: take a quick walk, do some jumping jacks, or stretch.

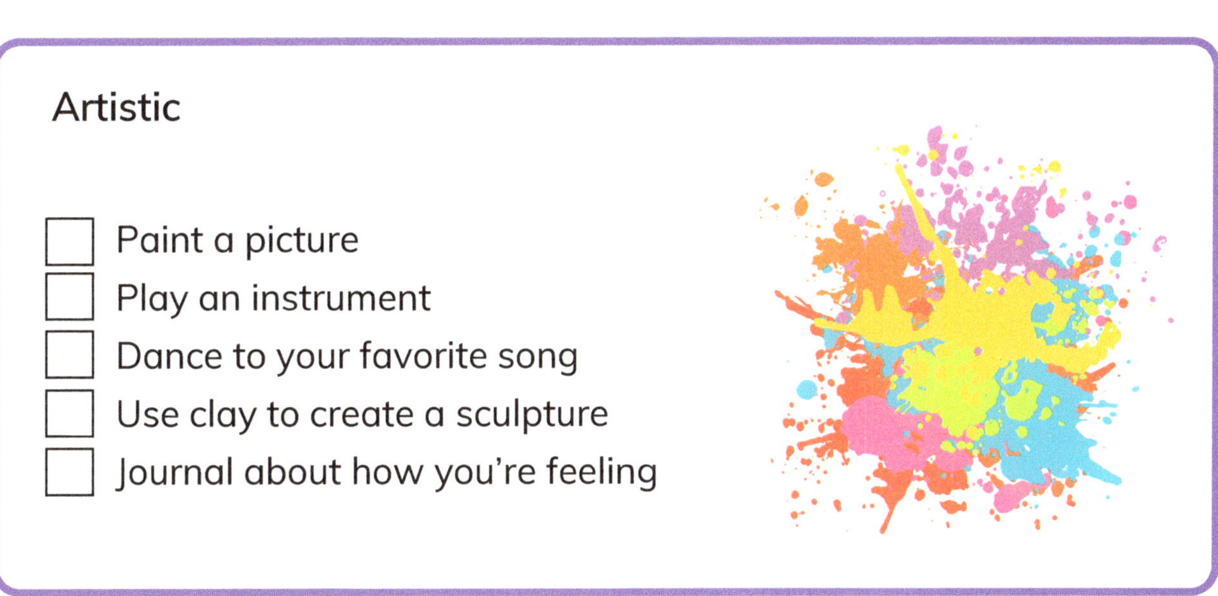

Artistic

- [ ] Paint a picture
- [ ] Play an instrument
- [ ] Dance to your favorite song
- [ ] Use clay to create a sculpture
- [ ] Journal about how you're feeling

Being different isn't a bad thing. It means you're brave enough to be yourself.

- J. K. Rowling

Self-Assessment

Self-Awareness Assessment

Name: ....

	Always	Sometimes	Never
I can name emotions I feel	○	○	○
I know my emotions affect my behavior	○	○	○
I can do hard things	○	○	○
I am special and deserve love	○	○	○

How often do you notice and name your emotions?

How well do you know yourself?

Self-Management Assessment

Name: ....

	Always	Sometimes	Never
I can manage emotions I feel	○	○	○
I can calm down my big emotions easily	○	○	○
I can set goals for myself	○	○	○
I can organize myself so I can find my things easily	○	○	○

How well do you manage your emotions?

○ ○ ○ ○ ○ ○ ○ ○ ○ ○

1 2 3 4 5 6 7 8 9 10

Not really. — Very much so!

How easy is it to calm down when you have a big emotion?

Relationship Skills Assessment

Name: ....

	Always	Sometimes	Never
I make friends easily	○	○	○
I can trust my friends	○	○	○
I can be flexible and compromise with others	○	○	○
I can ask for help when I need it	○	○	○

Are you good at working with other people?

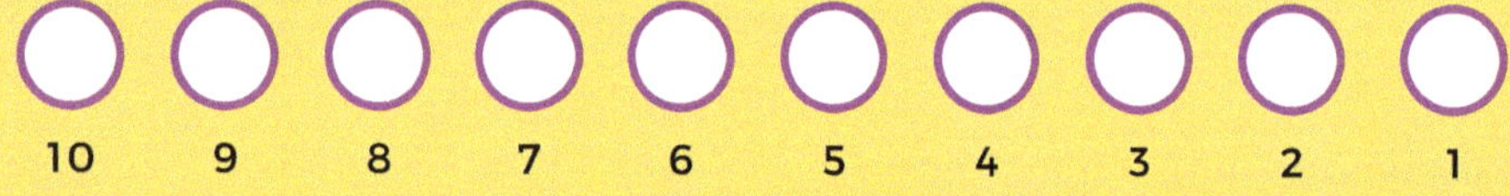

10 9 8 7 6 5 4 3 2 1

Yes! All the time!

This is hard for me.

How do you feel when you're with your friends?

Social Awareness Assessment

Name: ....

	Always	Sometimes	Never
I have friends who are different than me	○	○	○
I know others can see things differently than me	○	○	○
I listen to others to try to understand them	○	○	○
I respect everyone even if I don't agree with them	○	○	○

How often do you thank people in your life?

○	○	○	○	○	○	○	○	○	○
10	9	8	7	6	5	4	3	2	1

All the time! ... Not often.

How do you feel when you meet someone different than you?

Responsible Decision-Making Assessment

Name: ....

	Always	Sometimes	Never
I like to learn new things	○	○	○
I am a good problem solver	○	○	○
I understand consequences	○	○	○
I can make healthy decisions for myself	○	○	○

How well do you manage your emotions?

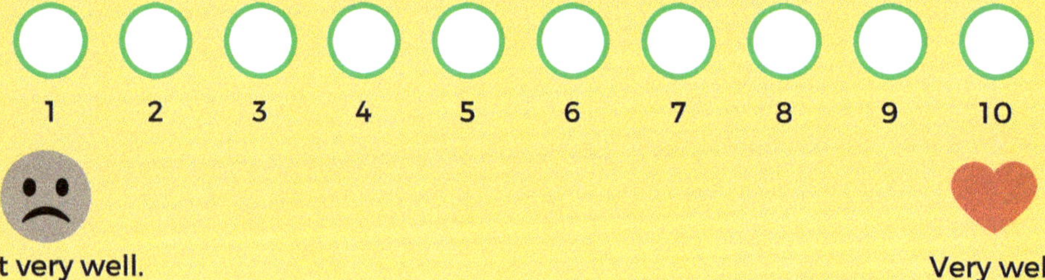

Not very well.

Very well.

How do you feel when you're given a challenge?

www.ingramcontent.com/pod-product-compliance
Lightning Source LLC
LaVergne TN
LVHW070408110826
845147LV00016B/970

* 9 7 8 1 9 5 7 1 3 6 9 3 6 *